DO I MAKE MYSELF CLEAR?

by

ARTHUR T. HADLEY

With Illustrations by
James Berryman

HENRY HOLT AND COMPANY

New York

Foreword

More words come out of Washington than anywhere else in the world. Politicians make words, diplomats make words, Generals and bureaucrats make words. If "words are weapons," as official Washington loves to remark, Washington is truly the "Arsenal of Democracy."

The words used around our own home with some effort and thought we can usually understand—"I'll be right down." "I did wash my hands before lunch." "The Smiths are such nice people we should see them more often than once every four years." These words can't fool us. They are statements we can handle. But the words uttered in Washington often seem meaningless and misleading. There is a good reason for this: They are.

I have been employed in the exhausting business of translating Washington words into English for some time now. The result is this basic grammar. Should any reader ever chance to go to Washington this book should give him some chance of escaping with his vote, if not his wallet, intact. This book may even help him make sense out of a political campaign, though my lawyer informs me that I am in no way to guarantee that in this introduction.

One more point before you dive in. Should any persons living or dead see themselves in the following pages I shall sue them for not recognizing my poetic genius. I haven't lived in Washington for nothing; I can cloud an issue with the best of them.

Contents

DO I MAKE MYSELF CLEAR?

CHAPTER I

A Clean Record

Politicians just can't understand voters. Voters are always clamoring to vote, especially on issues. Politicians never vote if they can avoid it—particularly on issues. They prefer to go into a back room with the elite of the earth —other politicians—and compromise the nation's affairs quietly among themselves. Voting is dangerous; it tags a man with a record. Politicians, like big-time mobsters, can't afford a record. To be able to offer himself to the people (to be selected by the bosses) a man's record must be clean and a record that is completely absent is spotless.

Before treating politicians too harshly, though, ask yourself this question: How would you behave if every two or three years your friends could meet together secretly and decide your fate without your ever knowing which ones had done it?

"I have no political ambitions. I consider it my duty to serve the nation in the job to which I have just been appointed and I will devote my life to this job I now hold."

I am running for Governor.

— o —

"There is something rotten in the state of Denmark."

Dig that quote. I'm educated.

— o —

"I was born in this town. I was raised in this town. I went to school right down the road and when I grew up I married a local girl. I held my first job in this town and I consider it a great privilege to run for public office in this area."

I have no qualifications for the job.

— o —

"He is a fine guy—an old friend of mine; but I seriously question his political judgment."

I hear he is planning to run a separate slate against me in the 12th District.

— o —

"I will not try to add brightness to the sun, luster to the diamond, shine to the apple, or give perfume to the rose."

Meet the boss of the 6th Assembly District.

— o —

"My answer is a definite and final 'No.'"

For the present I'm against it.

"I am still completely in the dark as to why the political lightning should have struck me."

Those $1000 checks were lightning rods maybe!

"Now, I don't want to sell you a bill of goods on this guy. He's not perfect."

I am supporting a known racketeer for office.

"I want to assure you that every veteran has but one thought in his mind—one emotion in his honest heart—the welfare of this, our most blessed, land. For we have fought beneath the great American flag and that wonderful flag, Old Glory, is forever fairer for the blood shed in its defense. We take no thought for ourselves. The only emotion in our hearts is gratitude that in the hour of this country's need we were able to volunteer—to give ourselves—to the defense of America."

After getting my case reconsidered four times I was finally drafted.

— o —

"What a fine man—a brilliant mind, a great grasp of policy, and a comprehensive knowledge of world affairs. If our party had more like him, we could stay in office forever."

He can carry his district.

— o —

"There is nothing in my private life that I am ashamed of, but will the voters understand political reality?"

I was caught taking $10,000 once as a judge.

— o —

"Yes. Absolutely yes."

If the pressure doesn't get too great, I'm with you.

CHAPTER II

The Well-Sewed Vote

The records have been cleaned. The campaign is on. Now the problem is to woo and win the voter yet save something for the boys. To do this the most important weapon in the armory of the campaigner is the wide, wide straddle. In business the customer is always right; but in politics the voter is sometimes right and sometimes left and the best place to be is in the middle. Another must is: Support your friends. A born politician is a man who after seeing a test hydrogen bomb explosion immediately thinks, "If that ever hits my district, I'll have an awful time rebuilding my old organization."

President Lincoln threw down the gauntlet to every campaigning politician when he said, "You can not fool all of the people all of the time." The secret ambition of every politician is to prove Lincoln a liar, just once.

"If my answer should not be entirely satisfactory, by all means drop by and chat with me afterward."

My plane leaves in ten minutes.

"I am for repeal of the Taft-Hartley Act, compulsory retirement at fifty, extension of social security, a two-dollar minimum wage and strong Federal regulation of the giants of monopoly capital that threaten the American worker."

I am talking to a union audience.

—o—

"I am for 120 per cent of parity not only for the basic crops but for all crops. History teaches us one thing—where the farmer is endangered, civilization soon crumbles. I am for free rural electricity, aid to cooperatives, increased conservation payments, public ownership of power, and better farm-to-market roads."

I am speaking at an agricultural fair.

—o—

"I am for a return to the simple virtues of the American Main Street and the unrestricted business competition that made America great. I am for repeal of the present crippling taxes, extension of the Taft-Hartley Act by a national right-to-work clause to guarantee that honest labor is not oppressed by unions; and also for liberal tax write-offs to help small business."

I am talking to the National Association of Manufacturers.

—o—

"I am in favor of everything I said before the union audience, the NAM, and the agricultural fair simultaneously and loudly."

I am drafting my campaign platform.

"We must never forget that one of the basic princi-
ples of our republican form of democracy is that the
right of the free citizen shall never be ground down by
the Federal government."

I had no time to prepare a speech.

— o —

"The overlords of the press and their minions have
joined hands in a vast conspiracy of silence against my
candidacy and what I stand for."

*I am not getting twice as much publicity as anybody
else.*

— o —

"It is a great pleasure to be here in this great and
historic town where the first coffee bean was ground in
North America in 1802—where the first commercial liv-
ery stable was erected in 1778, and where 704 soldiers
so gallantly served their country in sixteen different the-
aters of war, earning twenty-three decorations for
bravery."

I have a superb researcher.

— o —

"He is one of America's greatest statesmen."

He has been re-elected six times.

— o —

"I promise you one thing: I will wage a clean-cut,
above-board campaign on the issues. There will be no
mud-slinging, for that is not the American way."

I am so far ahead I don't have to worry.

"This has been one of the dirtiest campaigns in the history of America. No tactic has been too vile, low, underhanded, reprehensible, or foul for my opponent to sink to."

I am losing badly.

"In an underhanded attempt to influence the voters of this sovereign state, a sinister cabal of outside big interests has formed a gigantic slush fund which they are recklessly siphoning into this campaign."

My opponent is getting some outside money.

— o —

"This campaign is of such great national interest that little people everywhere have opened up their pocketbooks to give their hard-earned dollars."

I'm getting some outside money.

CHAPTER III

Two-Facing Issues

Sooner or later—the wise politician makes it as late as possible—the time comes when a decision just has to be made. In some hereafter, never-never land the dream decision of politics exists: "the answer that pleases everyone." About every three months some poor mortal becomes certain he has hold of this dream answer and will soon be President. As a result there are a great many counterfeits in circulation.

Ducking or dodging an issue is almost as dangerous as facing it. An issue has to be avoided completely. An able politician can see an issue coming when it is a cloud on the horizon no larger than a man's hand. He then either leaves the country on an inspection trip or works feverishly on something of vast national importance such as The Protection of Fur-Bearing Seals, leaving the dangerous decision-bearing issue to be handled by his less able colleagues.

"This is an issue that must be watched carefully. Nothing is ever accomplished by too hasty action and it is the great strength of a democracy that when an issue is referred to the voters, they, in their infinite wisdom, render a sound judgment."

This one's too hot to handle now.

"Unfortunately I have already given my word and there is one thing that is sacred in politics—your word. Once you break that, you're through. It is working a hardship on me in this case, but that's politics."

I've been reached.

— o —

"The world situation has improved so greatly that foreign aid can be materially reduced."

This is an election year.

— o —

"As a practical matter, we must never fail to take into consideration the political environment in which our actions eventually affect themselves."

I am about to compromise, with the help of a speech writer who's a Ph.D.

— o —

"A multimillion-dollar give-away program."

No money being spent in my district.

— o —

"I pride myself on the fact that since I came to Washington I have never missed a vote on the floor of Congress."

I'm too stupid to be given any important committee work.

— o —

"This has been a matter of principle to me since childhood."

It's a deal.

"Party loyalty is the basis of democracy. I am first, last, and always a party man; and I take pride in the fact I have voted right down the line for every program of my party."

I can't make up my mind.

"We are not only living in the times that try men's souls, we are living in the times that try men's minds."

I have inadvertently been reading the Congressional Record.

— o —

"Although the provisions of this proposed law are technically very complex, its purpose is simplicity itself— to aid those 297,625 small 8¾-acre hill farmers throughout the nation who now starve because of Federal neglect."

By a strange coincidence the technical details locate all but two of these small farmers in my state.

— o —

"As one Congressman to another, I want to tell you that was a great speech you made on the floor of the House yesterday—just great! I have been in Congress for some time and I can seldom—nay, practically never —remember any speech that got such a tremendous response."

He signaled me. He is talking to two voters from his district.

— o —

"This is a matter of basic American principle and woodshed honesty."

I am about to compromise.

— o —

"The voters of my district did not send me here to be a rubber stamp."

I'm too old to learn.

"This base program is one of the dirtiest and biggest steals in the history of our fair nation. I will not rest until the public knows all the filthy facts. And when these facts are known, this program which so gravely jeopardizes our national security will be immediately repudiated."

The boys in the Pentagon promised me a base for my district and then double-crossed me at the last moment.

"I am going to take this young man's case up with the highest authorities in the Pentagon. Surely the brass cannot be so cruel and so bound with red tape but that they can respect the constitutionally guaranteed rights of one fine American citizen."

A voter from my district has been court-martialed for rape.

CHAPTER IV

Corralling Committees

The real payoff for a legislator is not legislating but investigating. An investigating committee travels far, works little, and produces big headlines. This makes serving on committees the rich, full life. As the job of running the government gets more complex, a swelling flood of legislators finds refuge in constant committee probes. In 1947 the Senate spent just under $700,000 on special investigations—in 1955 over $2,000,000 went to the same thing.

With everyone in Congress getting into the act, anyone may suddenly be called before a committee. There is one easy way to avoid the unpleasant experience other citizens get into when on the receiving end—be a beautiful woman. Congressional courtesy demands that all women be treated as a cross between Helen of Troy and Your Mom. So if you are called before Congress, have a front woman. No Senator is going to stick a corporation run by Marilyn Monroe for back taxes.

"This is one of the gravest constitutional crises ever to confront our nation."

A Senator has been insulted.

— o —

"In the interests of a balanced Federal budget, it seems to me absolutely necessary that we in Congress lead the way in further economies. Much as I would like to have my wife along with me on my next inspection trip, I feel, and the committee agrees with me, wives should not be transported at the taxpayers' expense."

Let's get to Paris without our wives next time.

— o —

"I think, sir, your cogent remarks have elicited a line of inquiry that might well be pursued in greater detail for a few moments."

Now we are safely off on a false scent.

— o —

"I'm all fired up with enthusiasm about testifying here today."

I am the guy who got the investigation of my enemies started in the first place.

— o —

"I cannot tell you how much I deem it an honor and privilege to be here to testify before so distinguished a gathering."

I am here under threat of subpoena.

"It was a most interesting and informative inspection trip. My colleagues and I saw many things that caused us to marvel at the power of America abroad. However, we found evidence of some shocking waste. This evidence will be presented to the Congress and will lead to legislation that will save the taxpayers millions."

We have been drinking for two weeks in Paris on the taxpayers.

"I have nothing further to say at this time."
I am saving something to leak to my friends.

"While I want to be fully responsive to your inquiry, I am not sure I understand how the question relates to the problem we are discussing."

Do you suppose they've put a spy in my office or did they ask that by accident?

—o—

"You have asked what I consider to be the key question."

Thank God he doesn't know what's going on.

—o—

"I am receiving information from businessmen and labor leaders all over the country that the provisions of this law have proved unfair."

My brother-in-law is in trouble.

—o—

"After examining the evidence against him the Committee is unanimous in its conviction that he is guilty of grave wrongdoing."

No powerful friends came to his defense.

—o—

"With improved Republican management methods we were able to greatly decrease the workload in that office, enabling us to effect some very satisfactory personnel economies."

We sacked some Democrats.

CHAPTER V

Hark, the Tender Bureaucrat

The bureaucrat is someone not under political pressure to do a good job. He may work like a dog out of ambition, devotion to duty, an unhappy home life, or for pure enjoyment; but the heat is not on him. A bureaucrat doesn't think of himself this way at all. He feels he is a man whom everyone should praise for a good job, but who should never be criticized for a bad job, because that's playing politics with the Civil Service. A good bureaucrat lives by the motto, "Take the credit and let the cash go." Congress doesn't want to let the cash go and is hungry for credit. The two fight.

Some people don't consider department heads like the Secretaries of the Defense and State Departments as bureaucrats. They are though. They just haven't as good hiding places as the average.

"Unfortunately, the press has not been entirely accurate in its presentation of this affair."

I have been caught lying.

"Dear Mr. President: I want you to know how deeply I appreciate the privilege of having served in your administration. Association with you has been a daily inspiration in my life. Your appreciation of the great work started by me in my department leaves a warm spot in my heart."

I am being fired for gross incompetency.

"There can be no doubt but that owing to the interplay of economic factors there were several sharp price fluctuations during the time of active government interest in this commodity."

The boys in the know made a killing.

— o —

"I can assure you that the guide lines of the program have already been laid out in broad detail."

The whole thing you are talking about is news to me.

— o —

"I will not touch upon the great financial sacrifice I undertook when I came to Washington to serve my country."

My wife has money.

— o —

"Now, I have just jotted down here a few hasty opinions of my own on this subject."

This speech was cleared at the Pentagon, the State Department, and the White House.

— o —

"I had not realized before the Republicans came into office how much they had to offer the country. If you could get to know our present leaders intimately as I now know them, you would realize what magnificent men they are."

I am a Democratic hold-over desperately afraid of losing my job.

"We have completely revised the goals of the Department, rescreened all our personnel, and changed the whole basic philosophy of the Department's program."

The Department's name has been changed.

"We are in the midst of optimizing the already formu-
lated program. Our purpose is to point up several new
and promising directions in areas previously overlooked."

We have started a secret cut-back.

— o —

"While it is true that the world situation has changed,
one simple fact should never be overlooked. The con-
tinued goal of militant international communism is the
eventual destruction of all that free men hold dear."

More money.

— o —

"It is hard to tell just why they acted as they did in
that department, for what psychologist is wise enough
to put his finger on that instant where ignorance leaves
off and treachery begins."

In my case it's ignorance.

— o —

"We cannot with our limited vision now foresee what
God's future will bring. But we do have complete confi-
dence that, under the stimulus of the tried-and-true
American virtue of free competition, no effort or opportunity will be overlooked to put into effect, with all that
great power of which Americans are capable when
aroused, the vast power potential of the peacetime
atom."

A big program would cost money.

CHAPTER VI

Danger, Diplomats

A diplomat is a subspecies of bureaucrat that prays on foreigners. Congressmen, who distrust bureaucrats generally, distrust diplomats specifically. Both groups are certain the qualifications for the other's job are guile, an unfortunate accident of birth, muddle-headedness, and a cynical willingness to saddle the taxpayer with anything. To make matters worse, diplomats bother Congress with the problems of people who vote abroad. If the people abroad don't vote at all they get better treatment. Congressmen secretly admire Franco Spain and Soviet Russia as countries where the politicians don't have to bother with voters.

When diplomats talk about each other they do so in diplomatic language. Up to now no one has known what this meant except other diplomats and they have been too diplomatic to talk.

"The problem is not under active consideration now."
It was being worked on until five-thirty this morning.

— o —

"Protocol problems will be more pressing than usual during the visit of His Excellency."
He likes little girls.

— o —

"He is well schooled in the traditional arts of diplomacy."
That ignorant blockhead!

— o —

"At present we are in the process of preparing the strongest possible diplomatic protest."
We don't know what to do.

— o —

"The ministers have met to discuss informally among themselves the strategy for the forthcoming diplomatic conference, and have found themselves to be in complete agreement."
We got our way.

— o —

"The NATO Conference reached several hard decisions in respect to a few of the more difficult areas. In particular a close look was taken at the hard core of the third slice of the infrastructure of the SHAPE program."
The French are holding us up for millions.

"Although he has been in office in his small but valiant country for but a short time, he has already established himself and his nation in the forefront of the struggle for liberty. Not only his own land but the entire world is richer because he holds office."

He is here for a large loan.

"Of course, under no circumstances whatsoever would this government take it upon itself to comment on the internal affairs of other friendly nations."

The British have us on the hook again.

—o—

"The British came out with an interesting proposal at today's session."

How can they be so dishonest?

—o—

"He certainly is one of the finest examples of the military mind, although I am not absolutely certain that long experience in command is conducive to excellence in diplomacy."

Christ, what a temper!

CHAPTER VII

The Military Machine

Politicians distrust generals. They don't think much of admirals either. This is because when generals become politicians they usually get elected, but when politicians wangle a general's commission they just get investigated. This gives the politicians a feeling of inferiority, which they take out on generals as much as possible, particularly Army generals who insult the voter by drafting him. Don't feel too sorry for the generals though. They take care of themselves pretty well—though perhaps not as well as the admirals who can always escape into the middle of the ocean when the going gets rough.

Generals and admirals are the most undisciplined men in Washington. Military rules are so complex that they have to be broken to get things done. The generals and admirals are the doers and therefore the rule-breakers of the military machine. Try and give one an order some time.

"Man is basically a land animal. No battle is ever decided until the infantryman has brought war home to the enemy at the end of a bayonet."

If you really want me to tear your heart out, let me tell you about the old horse cavalry.

—o—

"In the next few years the seas will teem with atomic-powered ships of war. These invulnerable keepers of the peace, in the proud tradition of John Paul Jones, will be a valuable and flexible extension of U. S. military might."

Well, we have planned that way, anyway.

—o—

"A board of inquiry is making a sweeping investigation to determine and accurately fix responsibility for the accident."

Some young reserve officer will be blamed.

—o—

"While I have no desire to question the decisions of the President, certain purely military aspects of this program cause me to be gravely concerned over the future security of America."

The gravy is going someplace else.

—o—

"This project is so vital to national survival that it should get thorough and detailed research."

We will have an accurate answer for you after you are dead.

"I can assure you from years of experience leading American boys in combat that no matter what new miracles science may accomplish in the coming years, the basic factor in warfare will remain the morale of the individual fighting man."

I am too stupid to understand electronics.

"We are passing through a time of grave national danger. But it is also a time of precious national opportunity. Further, there are twin dangers. One, that through too hasty action we may be lured into a Communist trap. Two, that we will not seize fully the precious bloom of our opportunities."

After the secret stuff was taken out of my speech there was nothing left.

"While I am not in favor of restricting the necessary flow of legitimate information to the public in any way, shape, or form, I see no reason to hand the Russians vital U. S. secrets on a silver platter."

If the public ever learns how we bungled this one, we're through.

$-\circ-$

"Four-fifths of the world's surface is water and history teaches us that he who controls the vast expanse of water, controls the land."

Since sixty-seven per cent of the human body is water, admirals should control everything.

$-\circ-$

"I recommend that, in view of the grave national emergency that exists in this area, the office that I head be authorized to make certain personnel adjustments commensurate with the increased gravity of the national and world situation."

Promotions have been slow this year.

CHAPTER VIII

The Wild, Wild, Blue Yonder

The air force, like Texas, is a world of its own. It even has its own language. Ask an air force officer what he thinks about the situation in the Middle East and he will say: "I think we have been on the automatic transister system too long and it is time we let the flaps down for a quick turn into the flight pattern." Even callous Washington takes off its hat to a group that can becloud its position like that.

Right now the air force has horrible growing pains. All through World War II the military airplane was something built to fly home in on week ends and fight with if necessary. Now the military airplane is noisy, uncomfortable, dangerously fast, and useless for going home to the girl friend. Hence the pilot shortage.

"The accuracy of present-day bombers with their radar bombsights is phenomenal. We can now put a bomb in a pickle barrel at 40,000 feet."

The key word is "at" 40,000 feet. A pickle barrel and a small bomb are placed on an airplane. When the altimeter shows 40,000 feet, the bomb is gently placed in the barrel.

"In this nuclear air age the weapons of the future rank supreme. Against the vast, awesome might of the air force's atomic attack no aggressor dares make the slightest move, for in the atomic weapon we have an absolute force which coupled with air power gives this nation the opportunity of national survival."

The air force has finally reached its goal. It can destroy the entire human race without losing a single pilot.

— o —

"This program gives America maximum security at minimum price."

It's my trough.

— o —

"The guided missile will definitely not replace the airplane in the foreseeable future."

You can't fly home on the taxpayer in a missile.

— o —

"We have under way a detailed review of all our programs with the objective of improving their efficiency; always, however, with the fullest consideration to the matter of maintaining a high level of combat operational strength."

We are disregarding an order to economize.

— o —

"Some unforeseen trends have developed, but detailed evaluation so far substantiates the broad basic directions indicated in our last prediction."

We guessed wrong.

"This particular new airplane has several inherently interesting aerodynamic qualities and was primarily constructed to advance the state of the art."

We have spent millions but it won't fly.

—o—

"It is our considered estimate that the Soviet Union is not capable of producing an effective hydrogen bomb for ten years."

Whoosh!

CHAPTER IX

Smoke-Filled Lobbys

A lobbyist is a man trying to get people to do something you don't like. If you like what he is pushing, he is not a lobbyist. Then he is just a nice fellow going to Washington to let them know there what the folks back home think. That's what makes an investigation of lobbyists so difficult. The only definition of lobbyist the investigators can agree on is, someone influencing the *other* guy.

Actually, anyone who expresses an opinion is a lobbyist. However, when a man takes a suite of rooms in a luxurious hotel, flies in a planeload of ripely cute chicks, and then invites several Senators to an old-fashioned caviar and steak barbecue, with the girls around just to help people work up an appetite, even the other lobbyists suspect the presence of big money. Lobbying, like bigamy, is a question of degree.

"We had some trouble with the distinguished gentleman, but we finally managed to make him see the light."

He felt the heat.

"I want you to meet the admiral who is our new vice-president. The admiral is a man of vast experience, not only in battle on the bridge but also in the vast, vital, and complex field of industrial procurement."

He promoted the boys letting the contracts now.

—o—

"If the thought of a soldier's sacrifice doesn't heat your blood, then you are not right and you are not a real American. You are not even loyal to the youngsters you have brought into the world."

Open up those golden bonus gates!

—o—

"He's a man of great integrity."

He's content with two and a half per cent.

—o—

"He's a man of honest and good judgment."

He's a five percenter.

—o—

"He's a man!!!"

Ten per cent or nothing.

—o—

"I have known old Ed—the Senator, that is—for a great many years. He and I were intimately associated in Washington for quite a period of time in a variety of situations."

I used to drive a taxi around the Capital.

"He has only been in Government two months and already you can hardly understand a word he's saying."

The crumb won't help his old company.

— o —

"My daddy always told me, 'Sonny, don't give a stone to any man who comes asking you for bread.' "

How can anyone misinterpret a little ole $10,000 gift of friendship.

— o —

"The commission has been infected with politics."

We were voted down.

CHAPTER X

Gentle—The Press

Reporters, like Congressmen and Senators, are embarrassed about their jobs. Congressmen are called "Honorable," reporters "Gentlemen of the Press." Pawnbrokers, tree surgeons, plumbers, and other really honorable occupations don't have to bother with such reminders. There is a good deal of debate, some of it friendly, about the place of the press. Most of the noise is made by people who are in the news and want out, or out of the news and want in. The second group is much larger. To take care of them all sorts of newspapers, magazines, and television programs have sprung up. Some of them even carry news.

Reporters know less about what's going on in Washington than anyone else. A man will talk over his problems with a total stranger in a bar, but he won't tell an old friend who is a reporter. This phenomenon is known as the "power of the press."

"Never in my long years as a reporter have I seen freedom of the press so endangered as now."

I have just been scooped.

—o—

"Our Moscow correspondent reports——"

Radio London said yesterday——

—o—

"Reliable sources indicate the following to be true."

Some rumors claim——

—o—

"A report that John Jones is honest has yet to be denied officially."

We have been forced to retract our story calling John Jones a liar.

—o—

"The people will not rest until the official responsible for this vast confusion is brought to light."

One of our reporters got his facts mixed.

—o—

"I want to protest against the scandalous leaks and dangerous breeches of secrecy that have occurred in the past few weeks."

Other papers are getting news we aren't.

—o—

"Point of order, Mr. Chairman, point of order."

Any Washingtonian stupid enough to comment on this in the public press is an imposter.

"We are going to give this story fuller play—a completely unbiased treatment hitting both sides of the question hard."

Our advertisers want us to slant this story another way.

CHAPTER XI

That Makes It Legal

Washington lawyers are a race apart. This is not just because nobody else will talk to them. Part of it is the peculiarity of their jobs. In government, law is made by the public, not the courts. A Washington case may be tried in court, but usually that fiction is done away with and the case argued somewhere in Congress with such legal niceties as rules of evidence dispensed with. This makes a Washington lawyer basically a lobbyist with a union card.

The first reaction of an ordinary lawyer to a problem is, "What's the law?" The first reaction of a Washington lawyer is, "Who's handling this?" For Washington is not the know-how town but the know-who town. The elite of know-who's are Washington lawyers.

"THERE, that makes it legal."

We thought we'd never get him to sign that one. (Should never be confused with "That makes it legal" above.)

"I think we need a bit more balance in the ranks of the distinguished counsel that will represent us in the matter."

I have just noticed that all our lawyers are Democrats.

—o—

"I am not familiar with the statement made by the distinguished gentleman which is receiving such undivided attention here."

If I were to recite it backward rapidly in Hindustani I might stutter.

—o—

"I cannot be quite certain, but it is my belief that Mr. Jones participated in the decision.

Honestly, we didn't do it.

—o—

"You can count on my client's wholehearted cooperation."

Just try and pin him down.

—o—

"Counsel."

Any lawyer.

—o—

"Distinguished counsel."

Any Washington lawyer.

"Most Honorable and distinguished counsel."
Any ex-Congressman now a Washington lawyer.

"That makes it legal."

Eleven of our eighteen partners think you can get away with this and we are going to charge you $40,000 for this advice."

—o—

"This will be legal."

We know someone on the committee—never to be confused with the two statements above.